# Drawing Your First Fairy: Book Of Expert Techniques

Illustrative Guide to Making Your Own Fairy Book

Fairy Book

By : Gala Publication

Published By :

Gala Publication



ISBN-13: **978-1522708964**
ISBN-10: **1522708960**

# Table of Contents

**Learn To Draw Fairy 6 Characters:...........................**
**Learn To Draw Cartoon Fairy....................................**
**Learn To Draw Evil Fairy ..........................................**
**Learn To Draw Mischievous Fairy...........................**
**Learn To Draw Skull Fairy.........................................**
**Learn To Draw Tiger Fairy........................................**
**Learn To Draw Tinkerbell Fairy...............................**

# CARTOON FAIRY

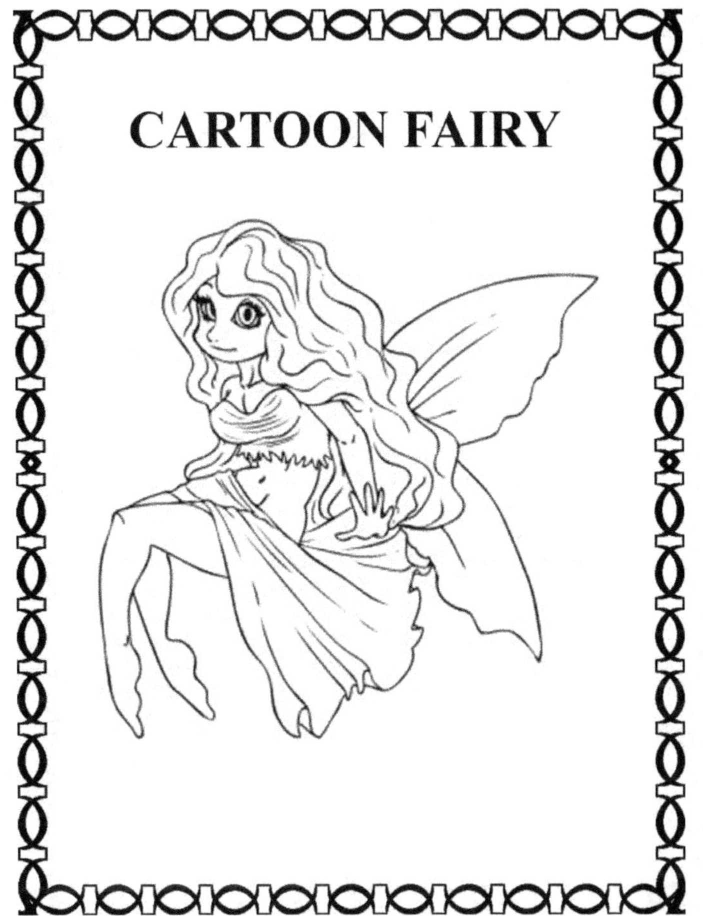

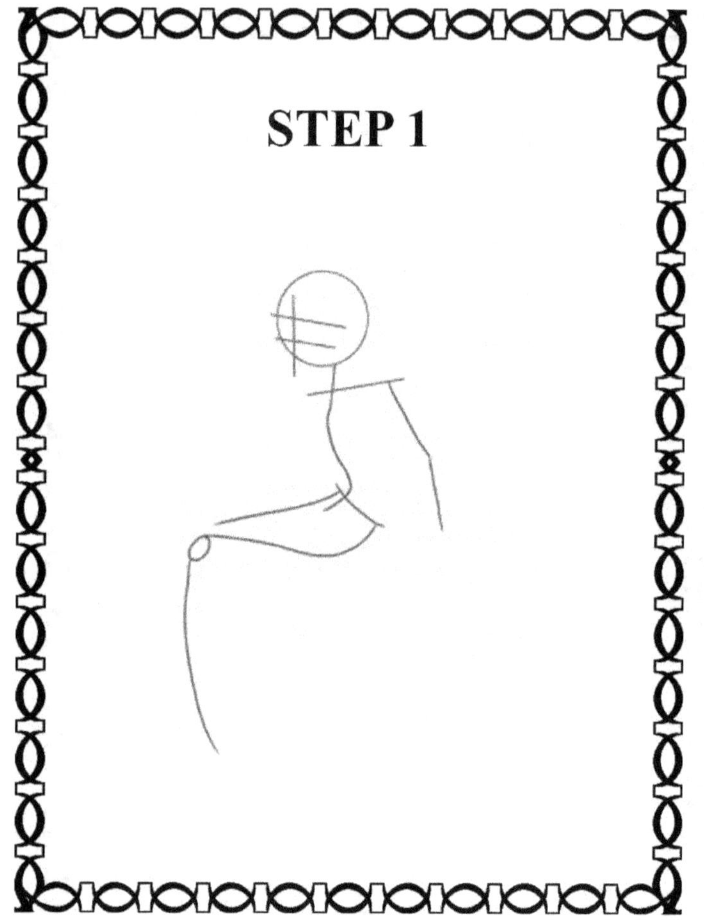
STEP 1

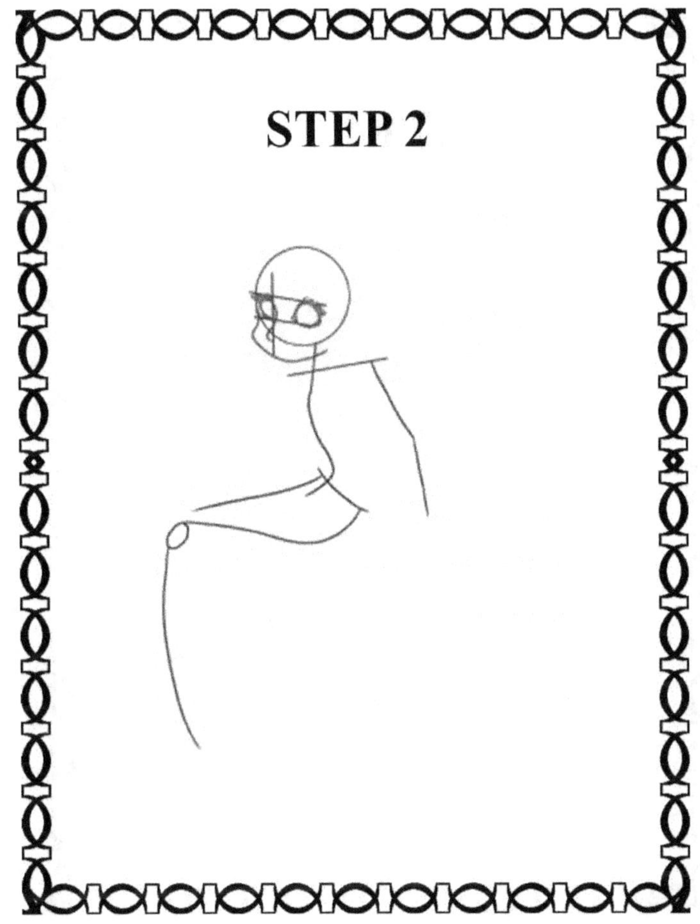
STEP 2

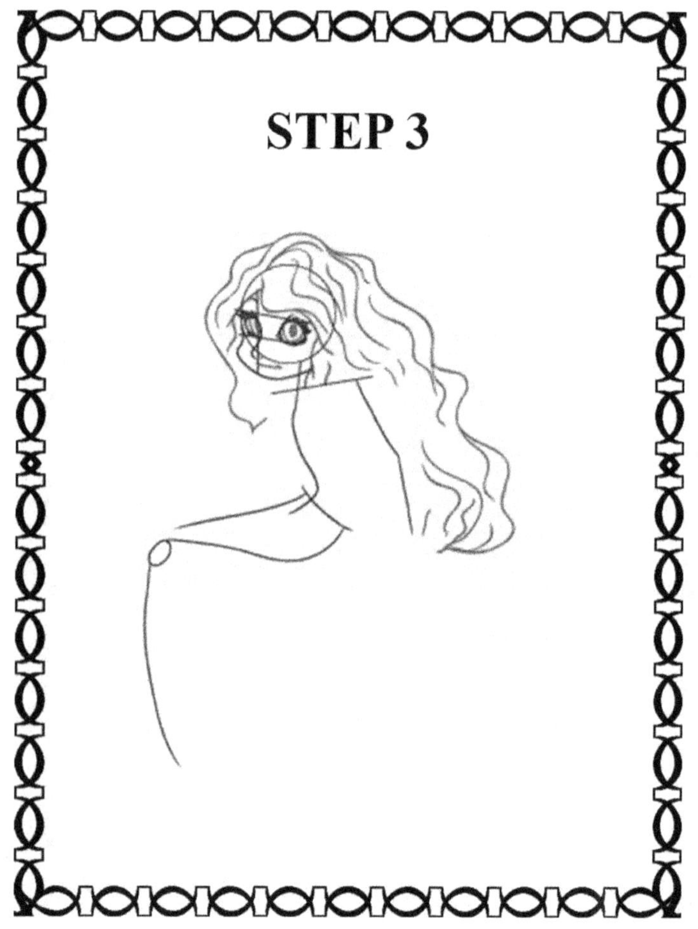
STEP 3

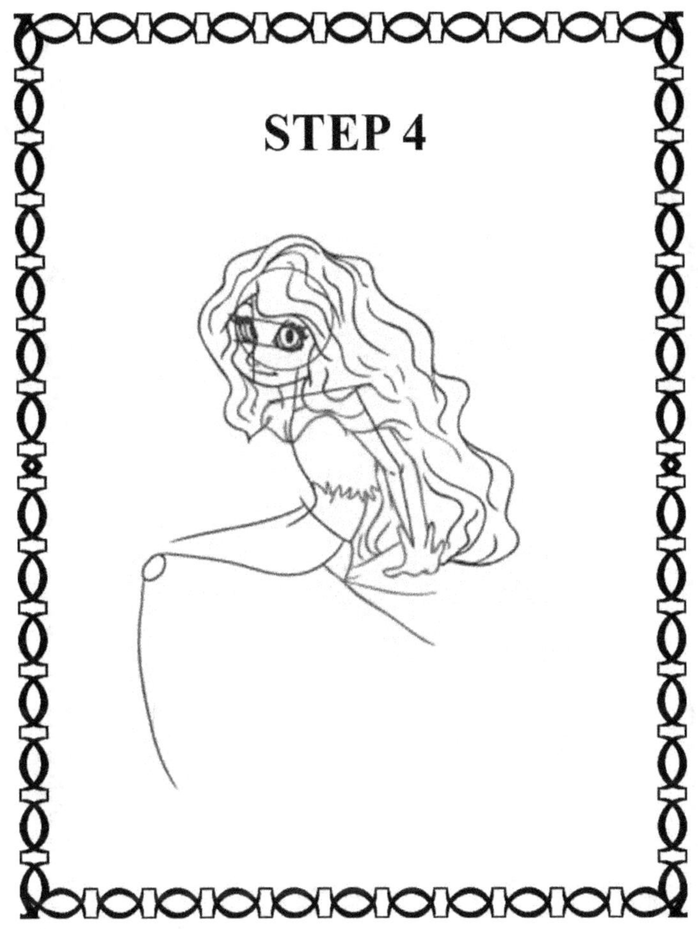
STEP 4

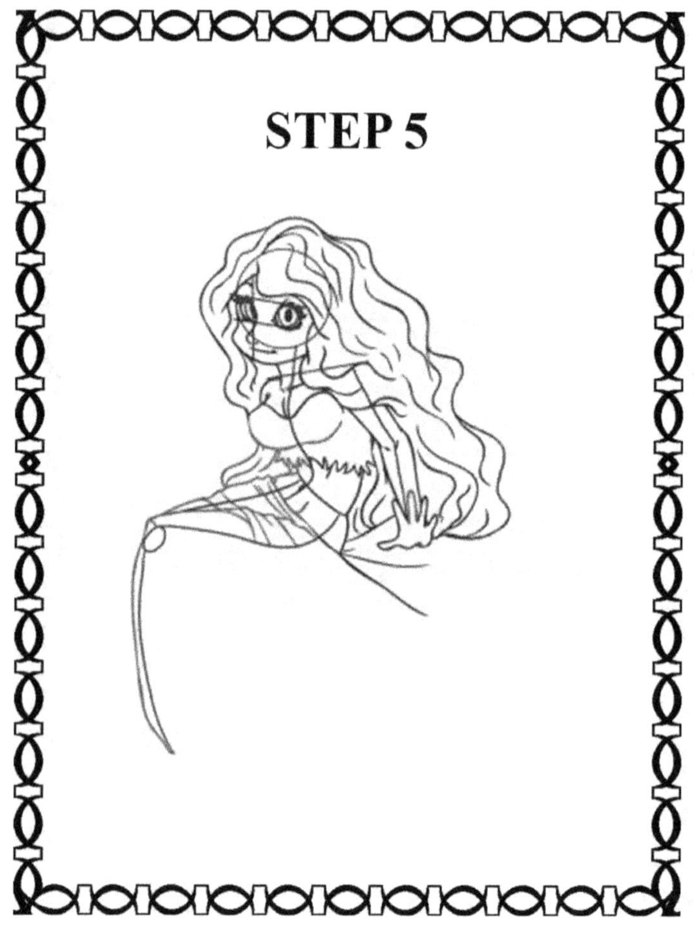
STEP 5

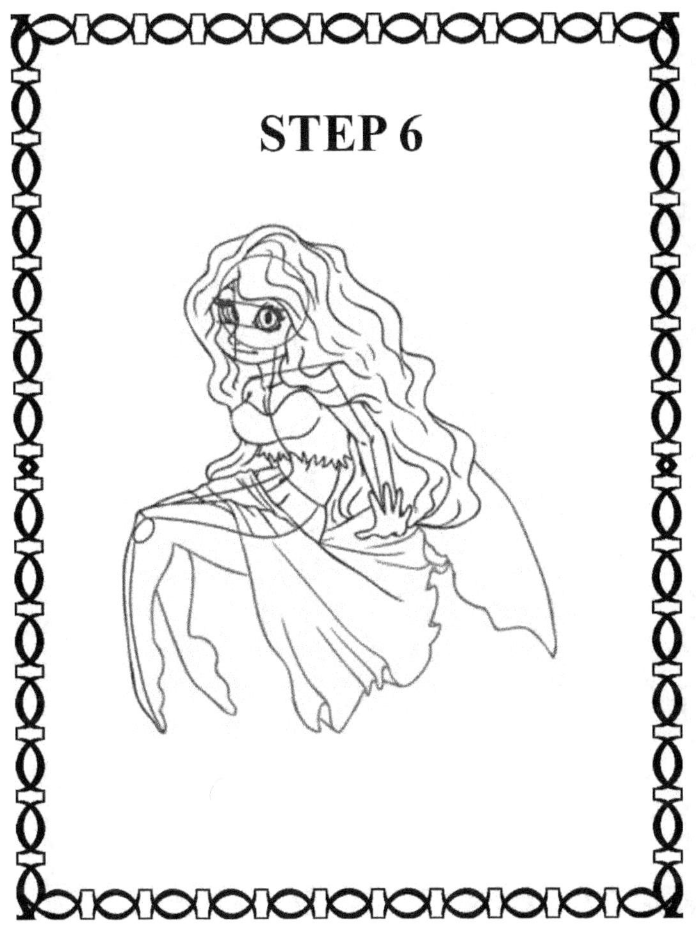
STEP 6

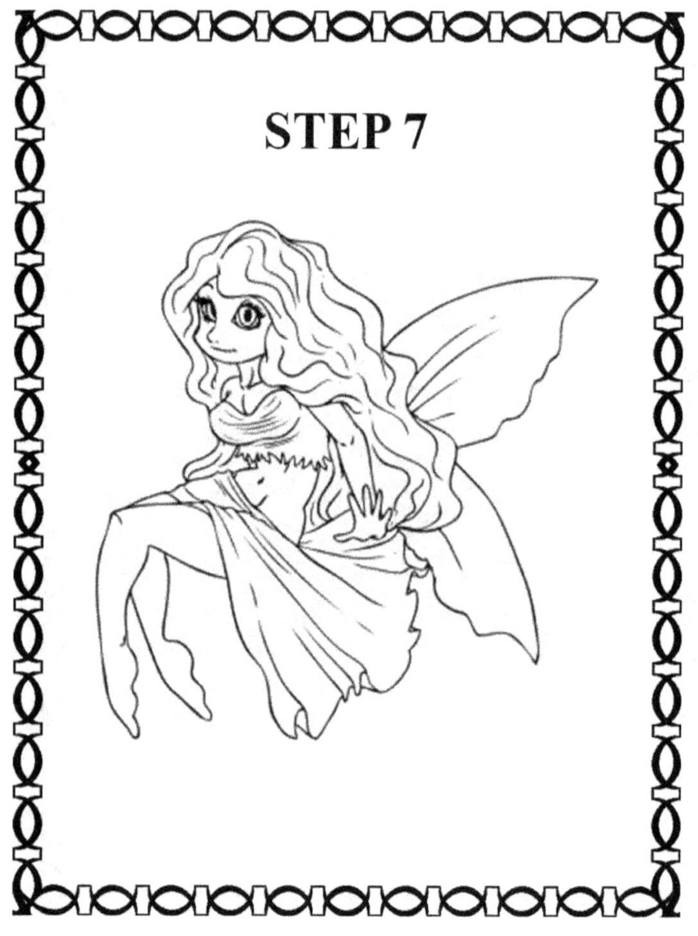
STEP 7

# EVIL FAIRY

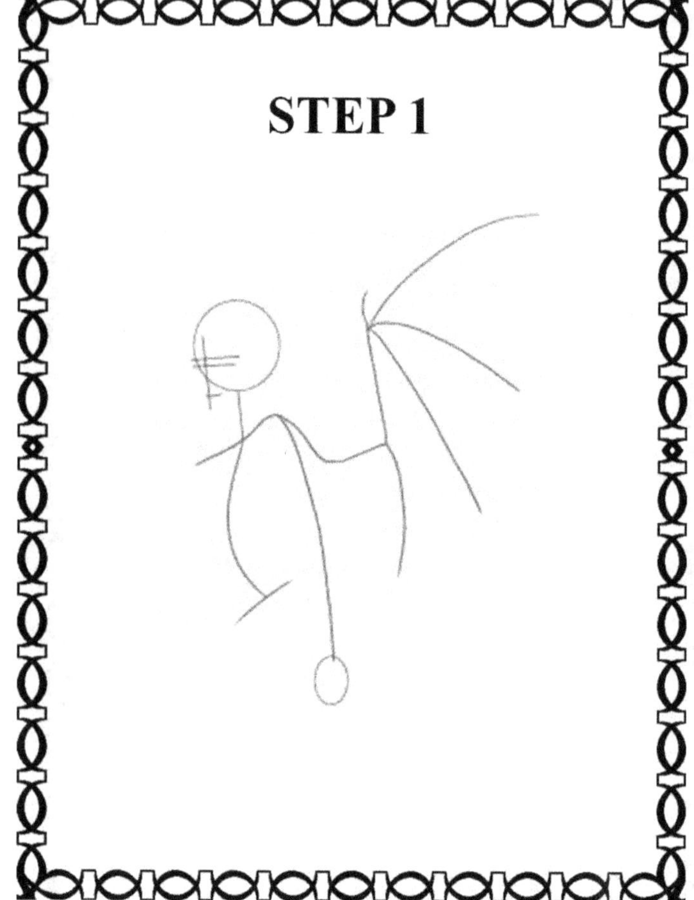
STEP 1

# STEP 2

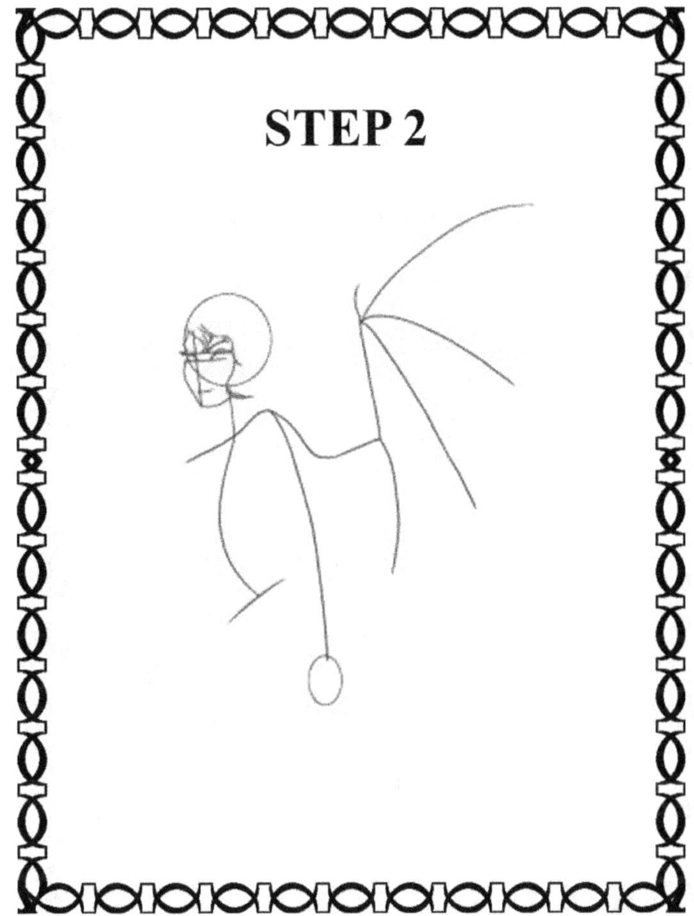

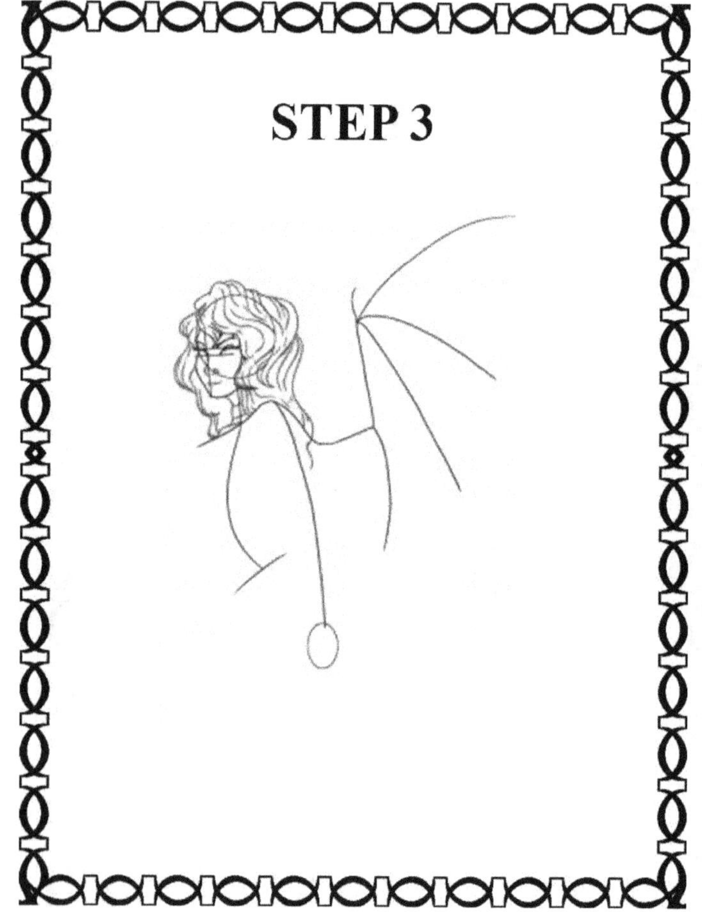
STEP 3

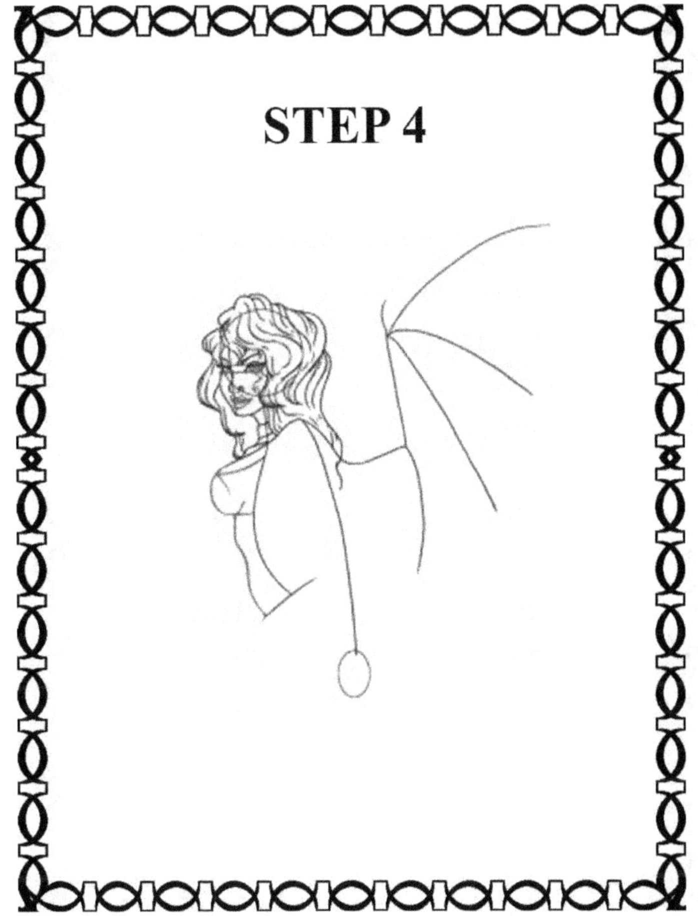
STEP 4

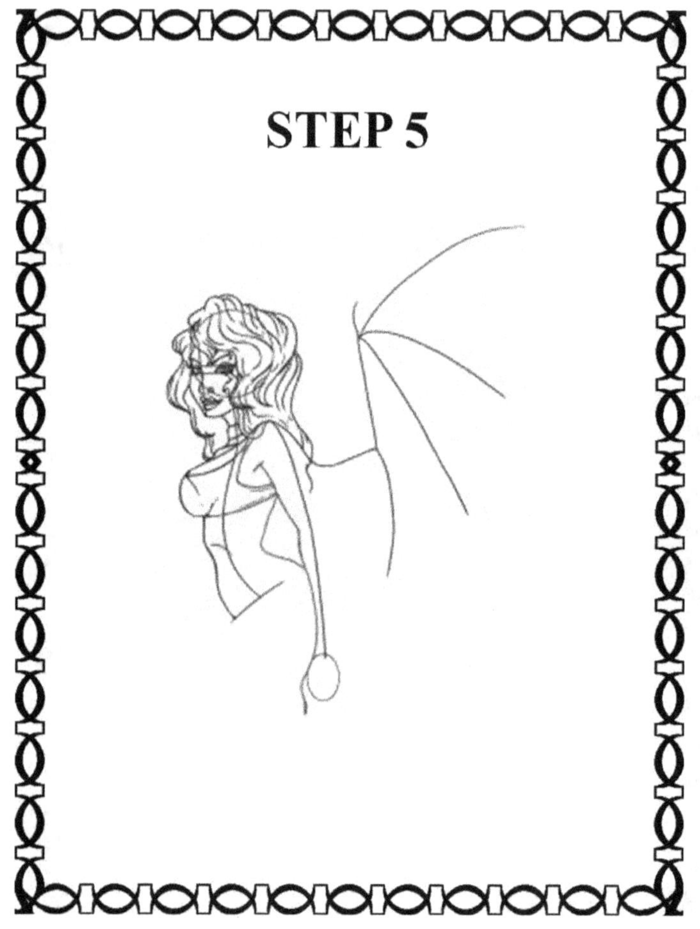
STEP 5

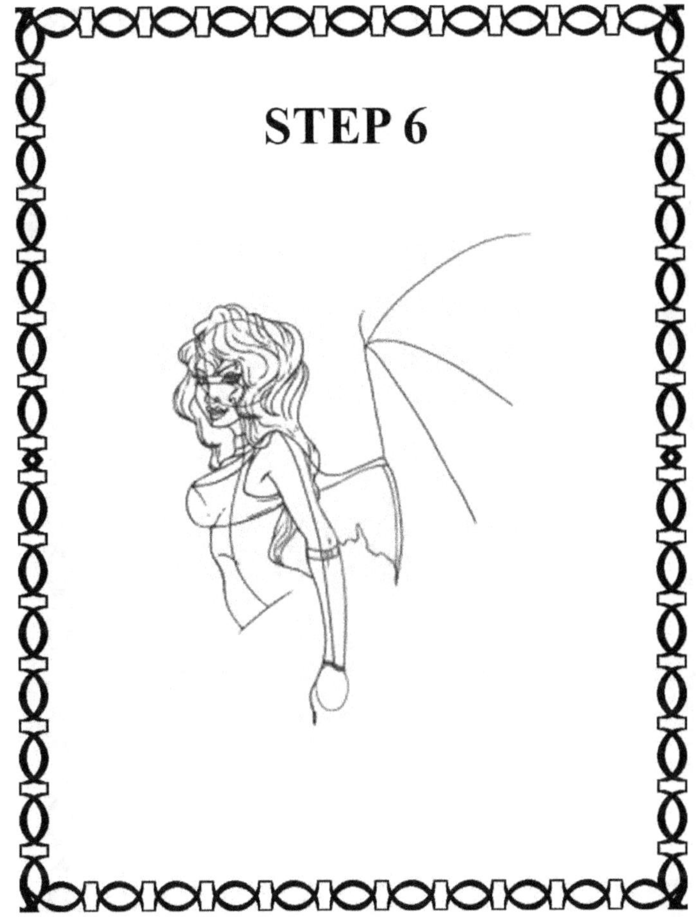
STEP 6

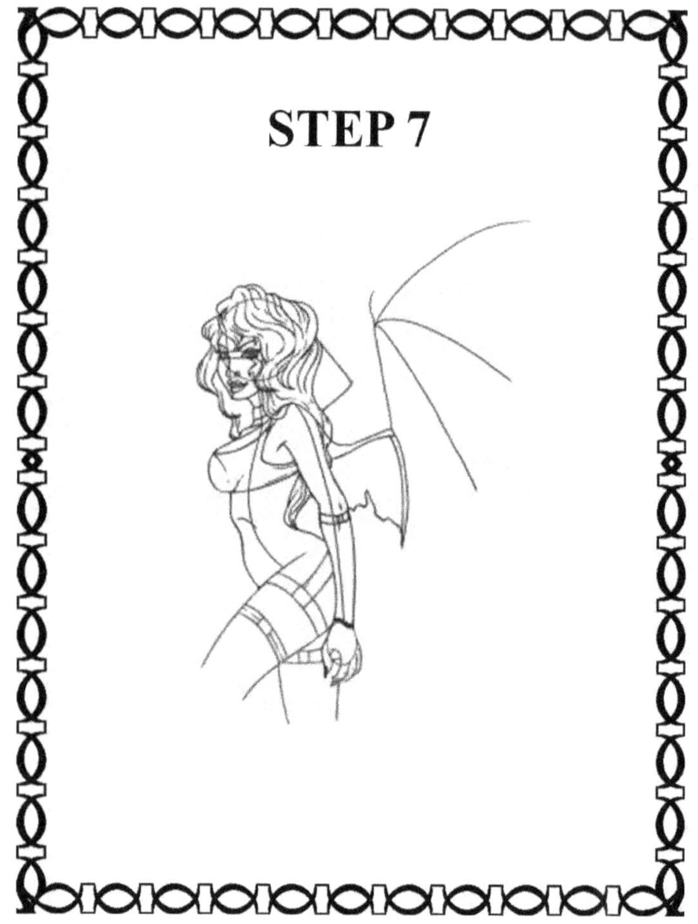
STEP 7

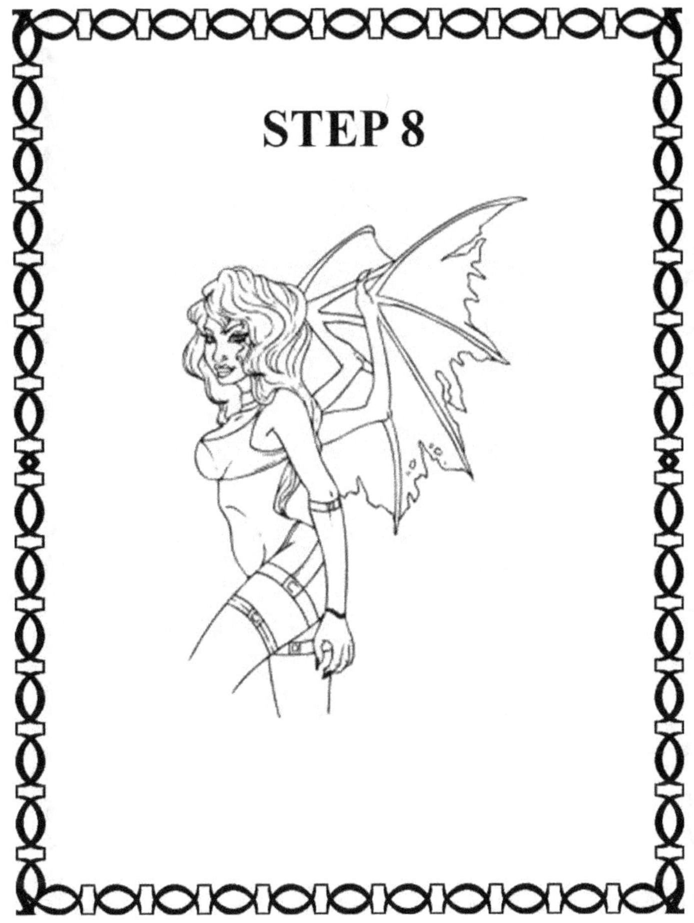
STEP 8

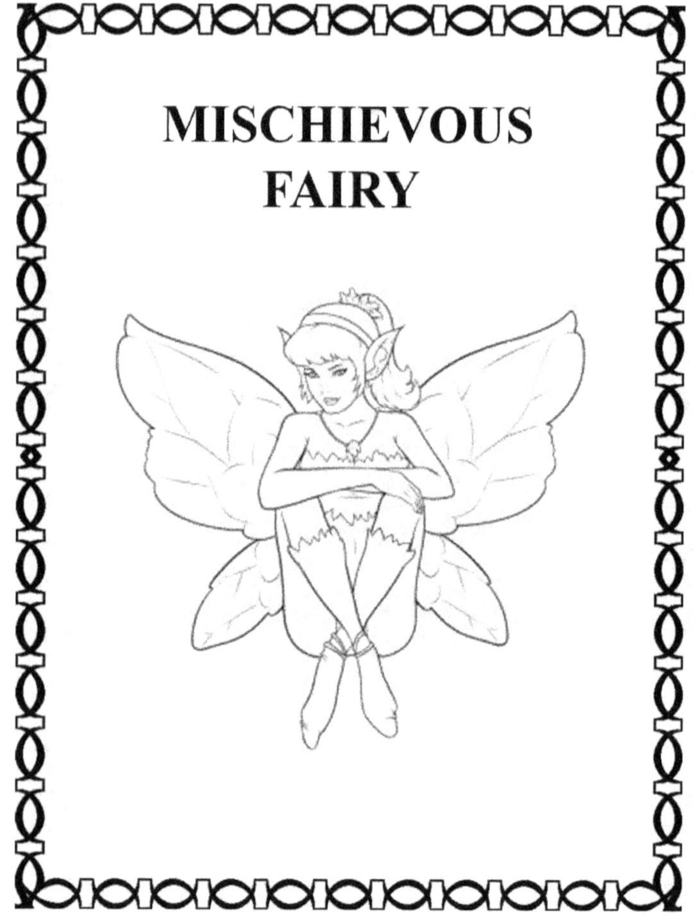
MISCHIEVOUS
FAIRY

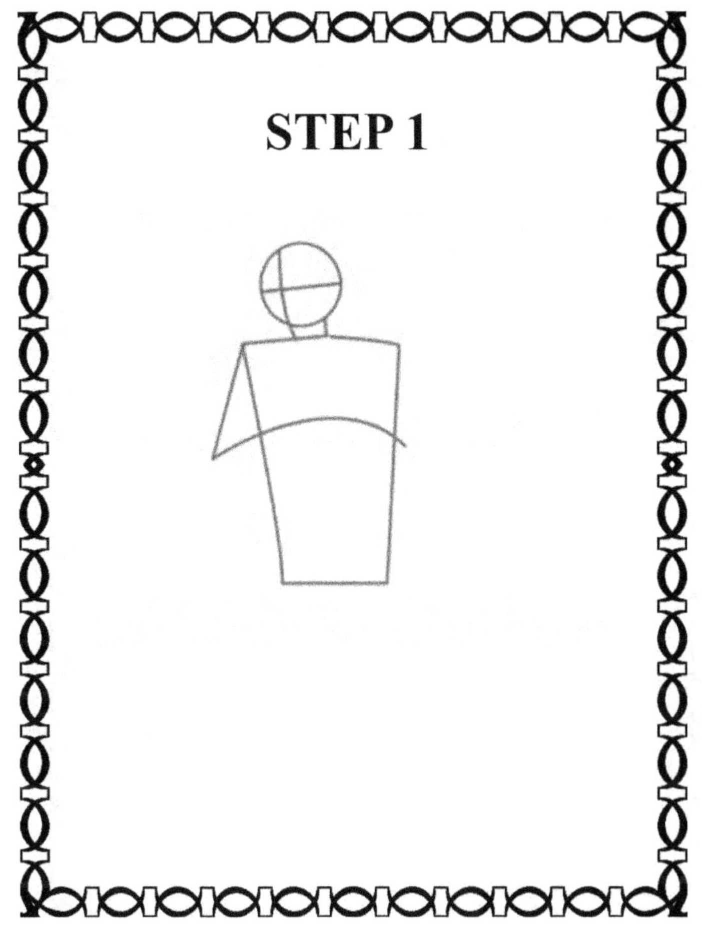
STEP 1

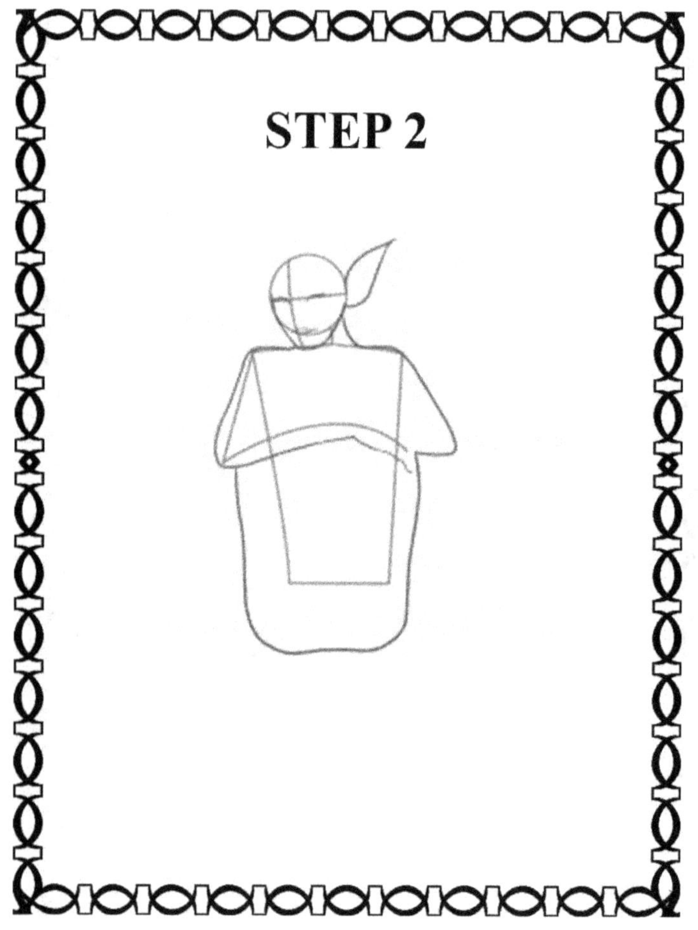
STEP 2

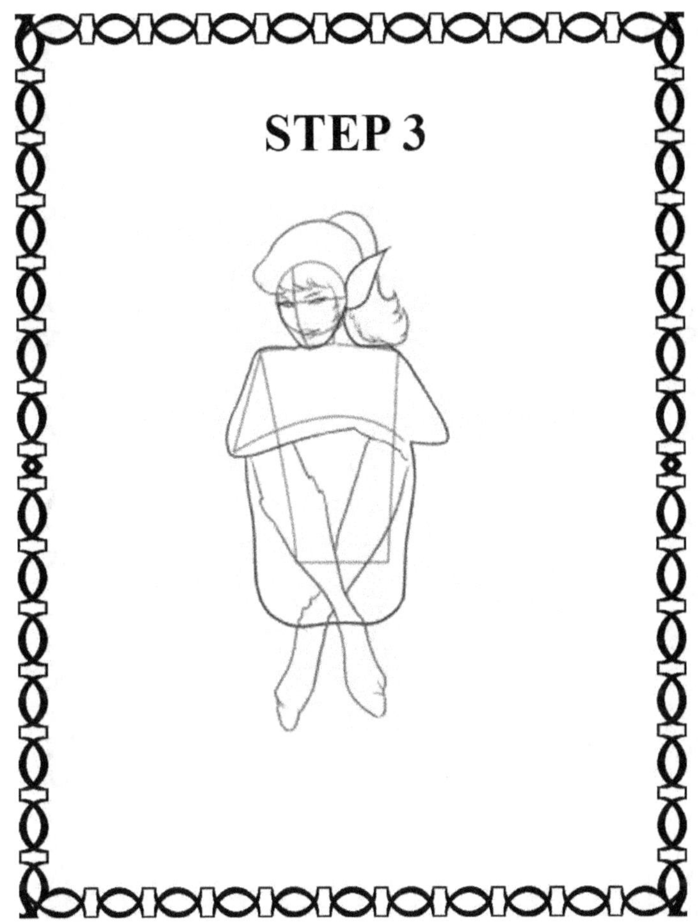
STEP 3

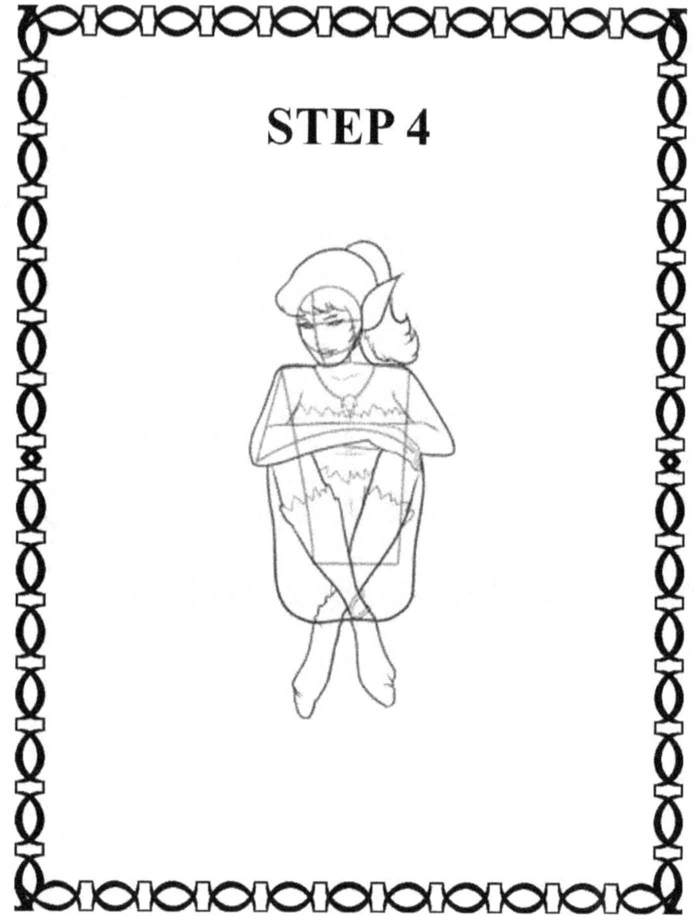
STEP 4

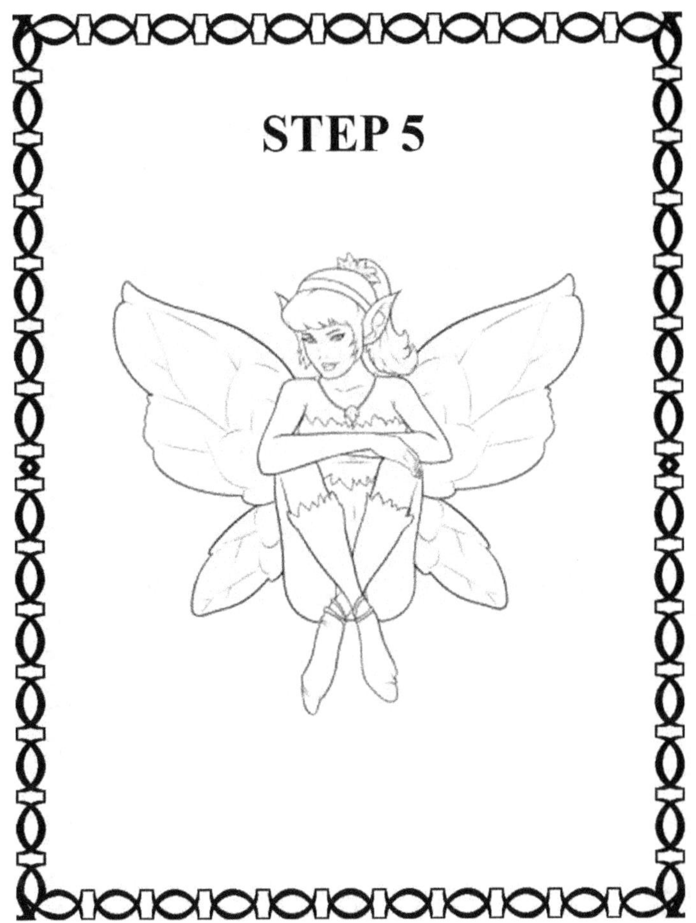
STEP 5

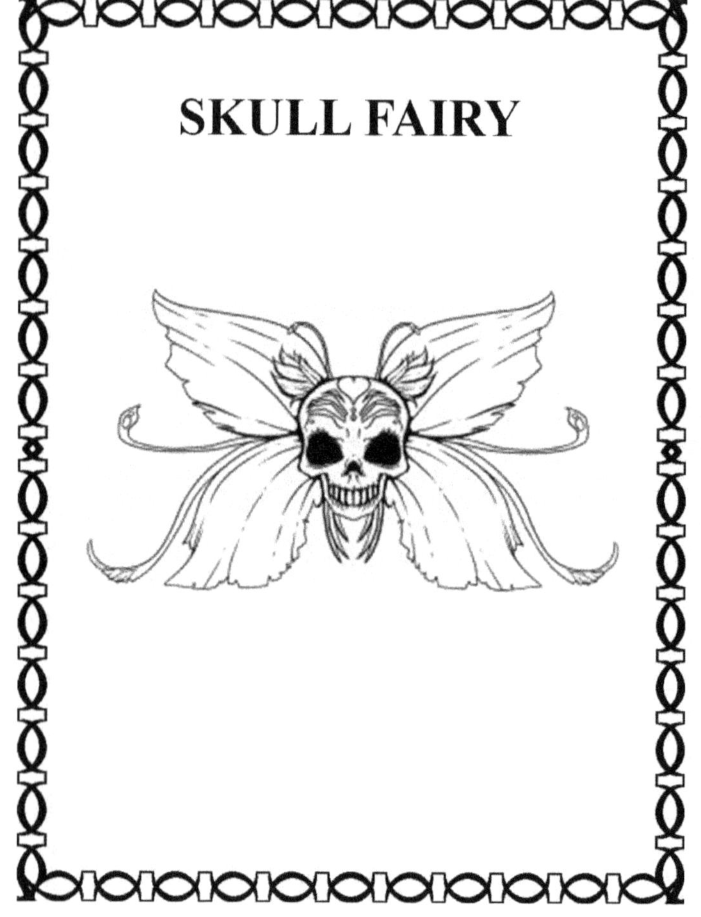
SKULL FAIRY

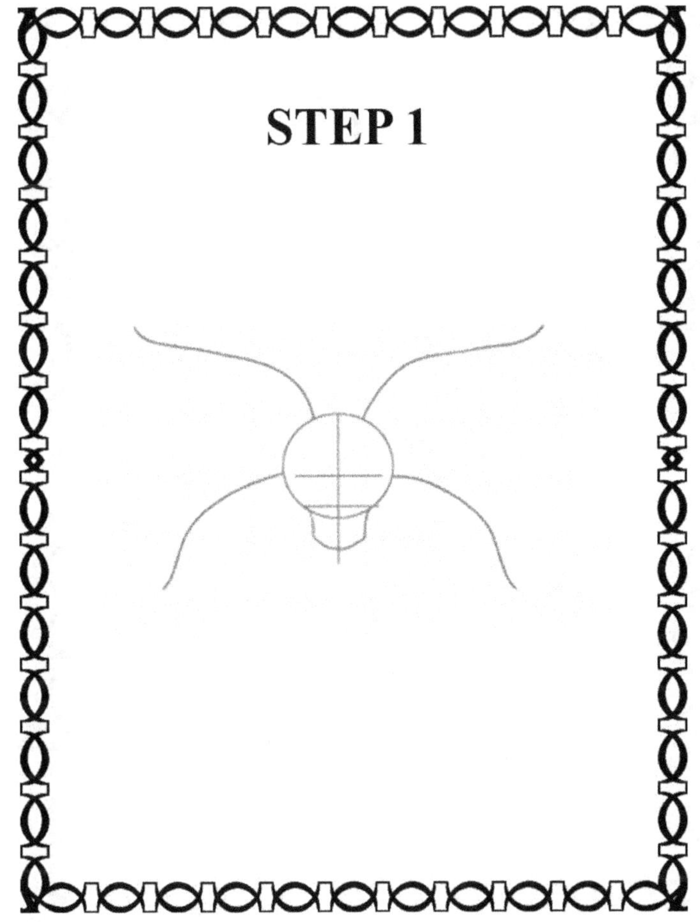
STEP 1

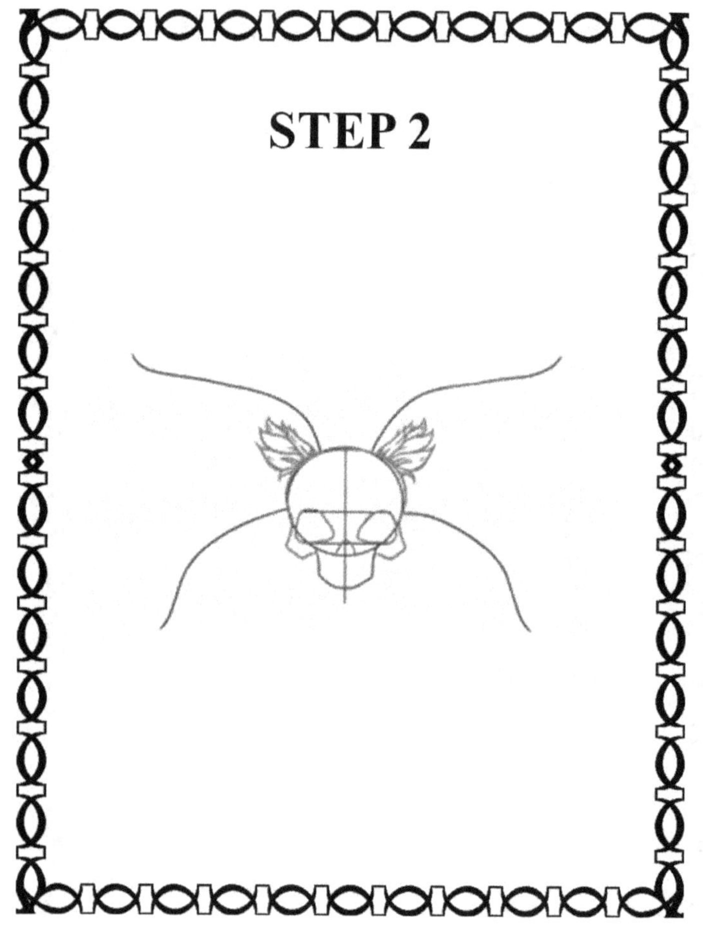
STEP 2

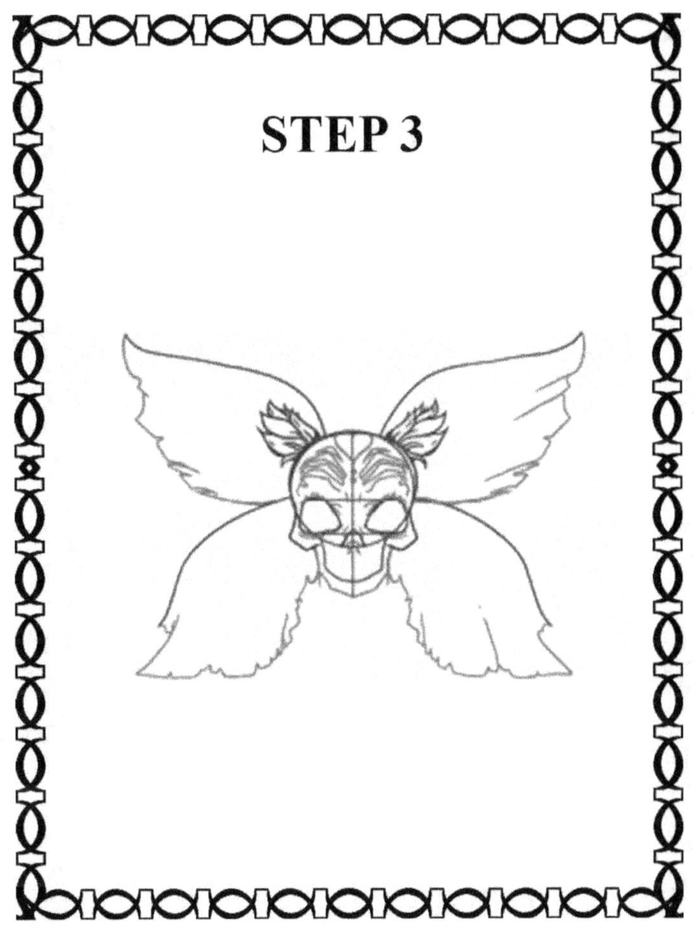
STEP 3

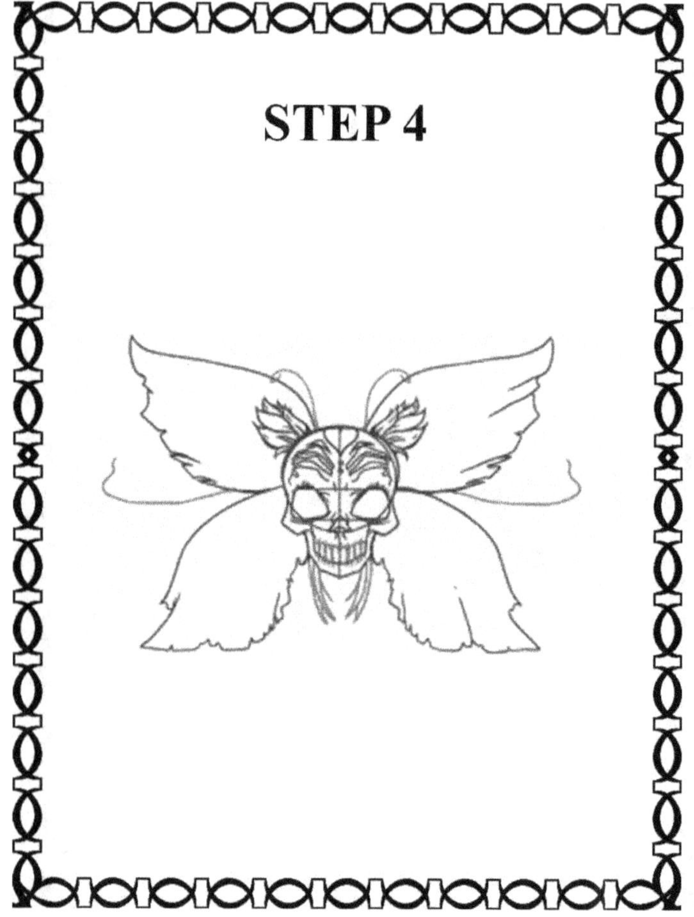
STEP 4

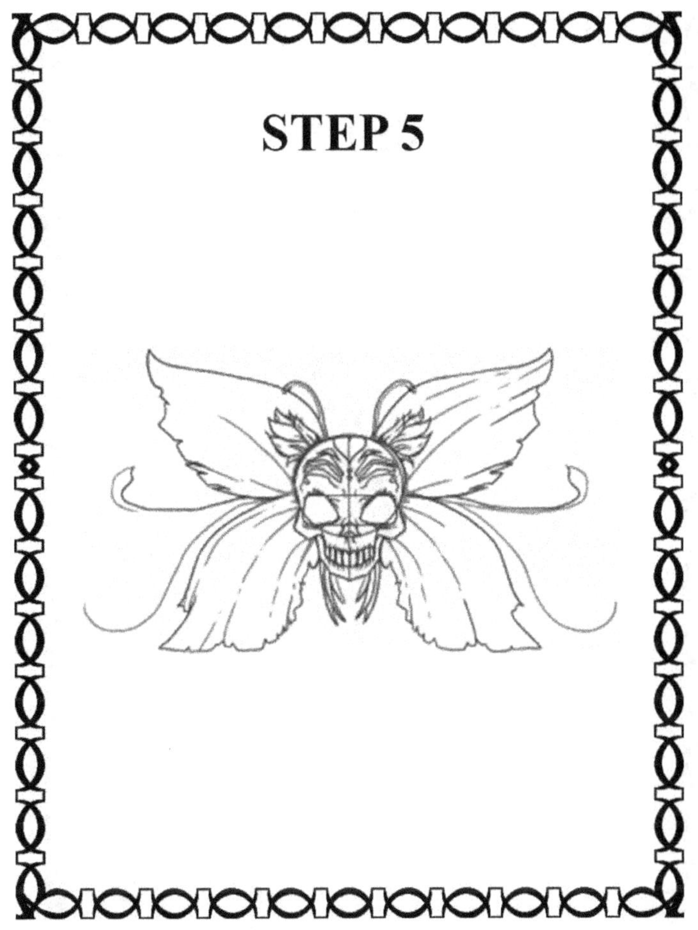
STEP 5

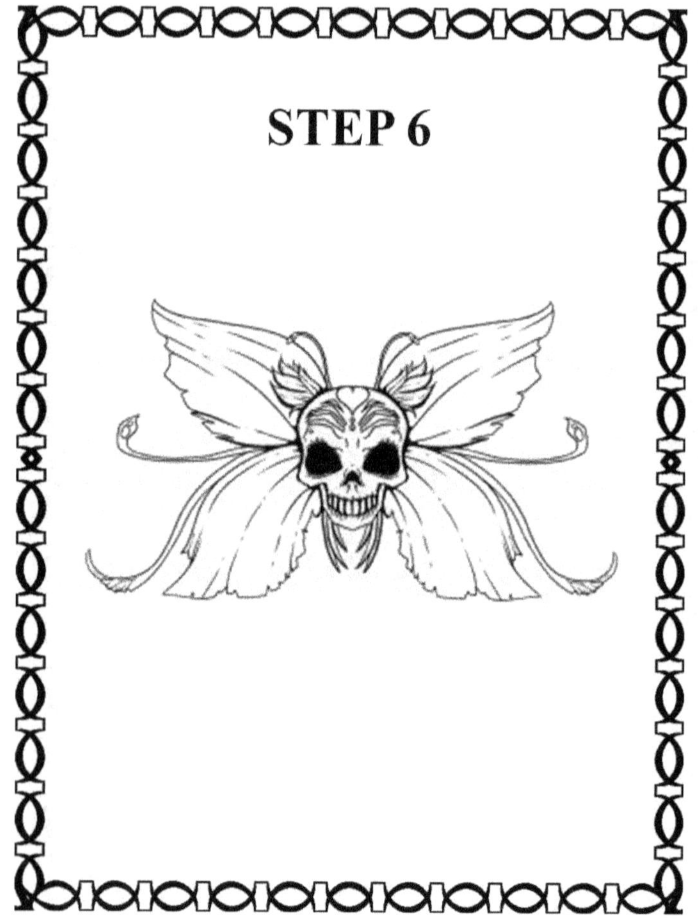
STEP 6

# TIGER FAIRY

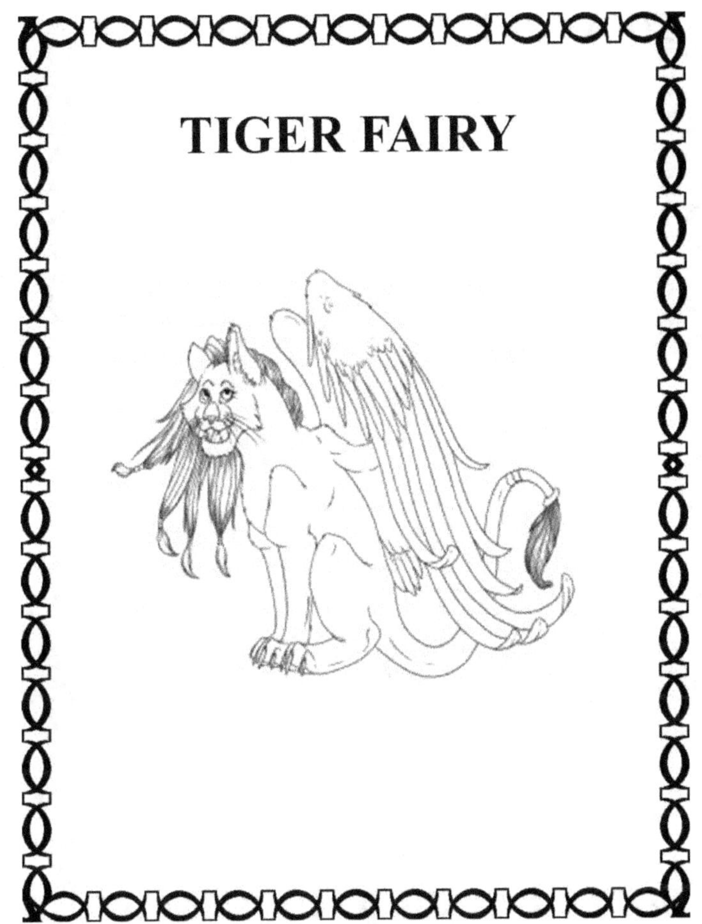

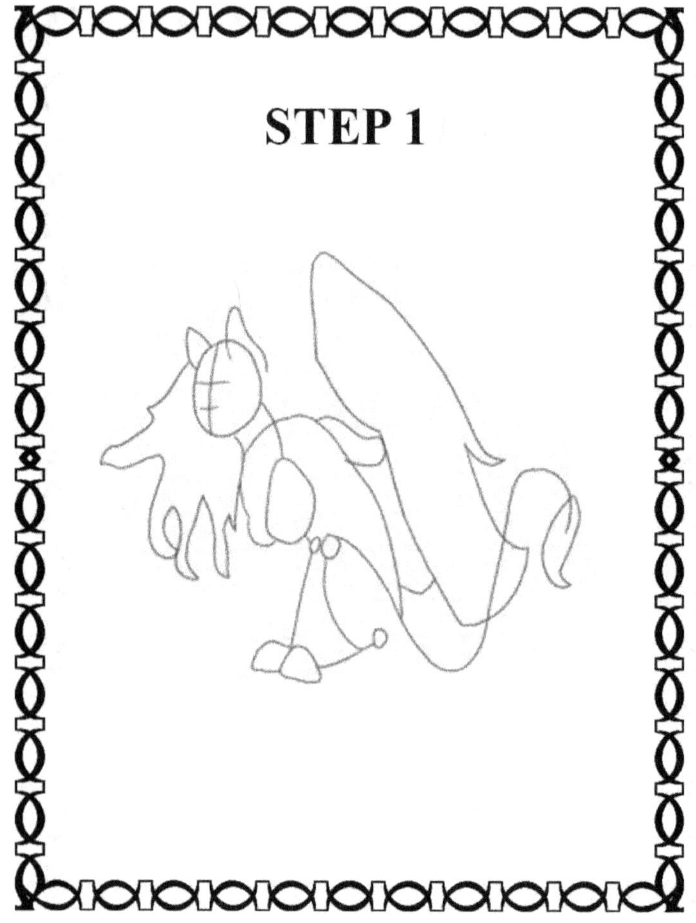
STEP 1

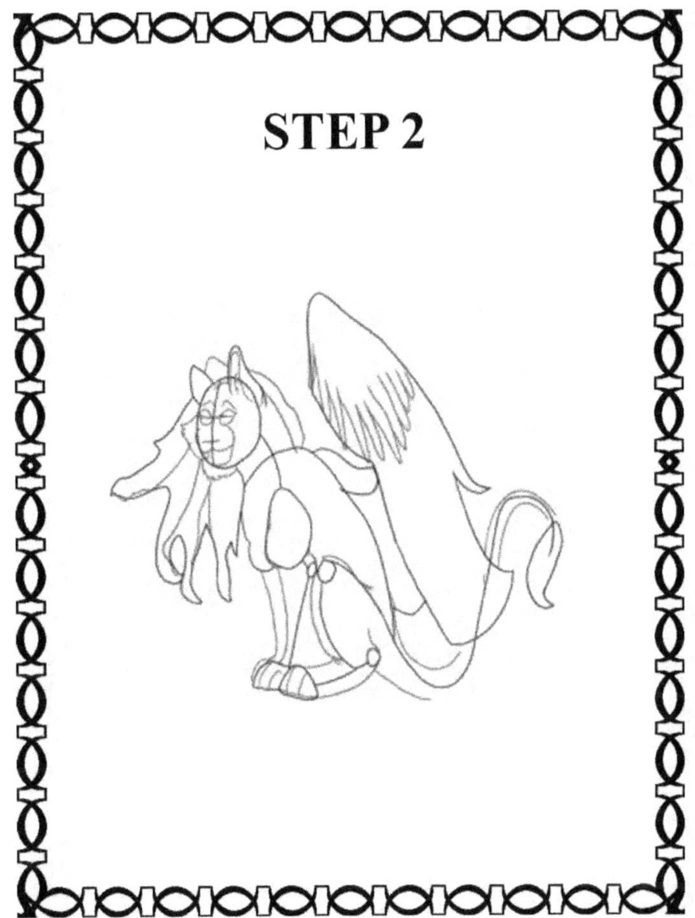
STEP 2

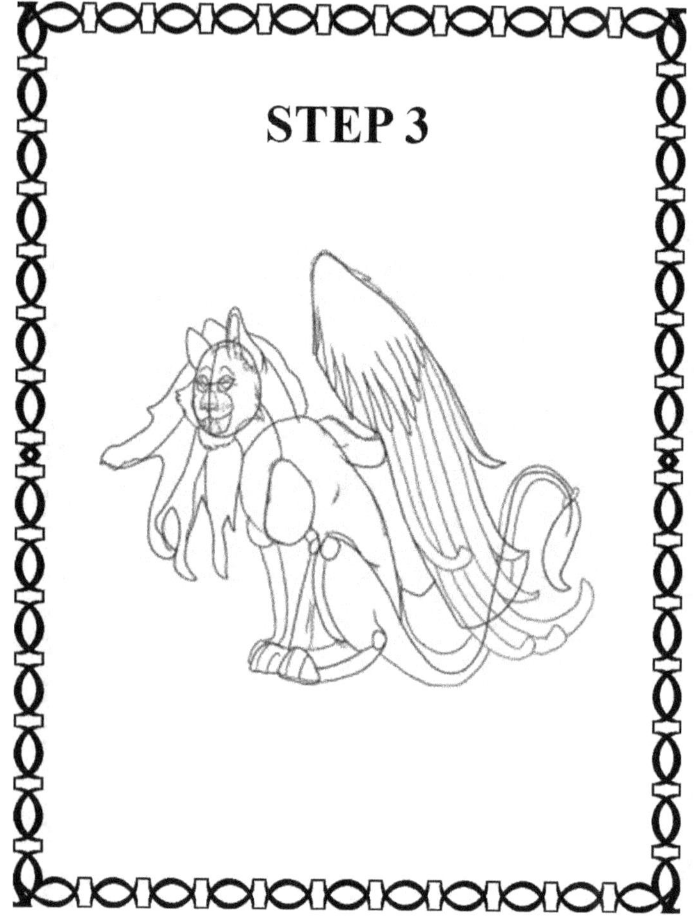
STEP 3

# STEP 4

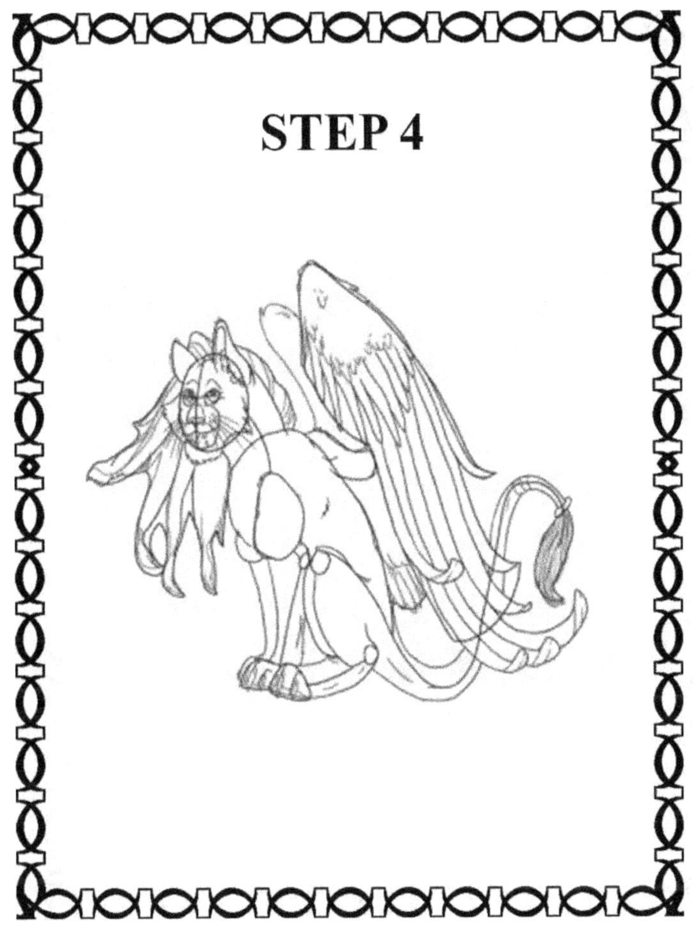

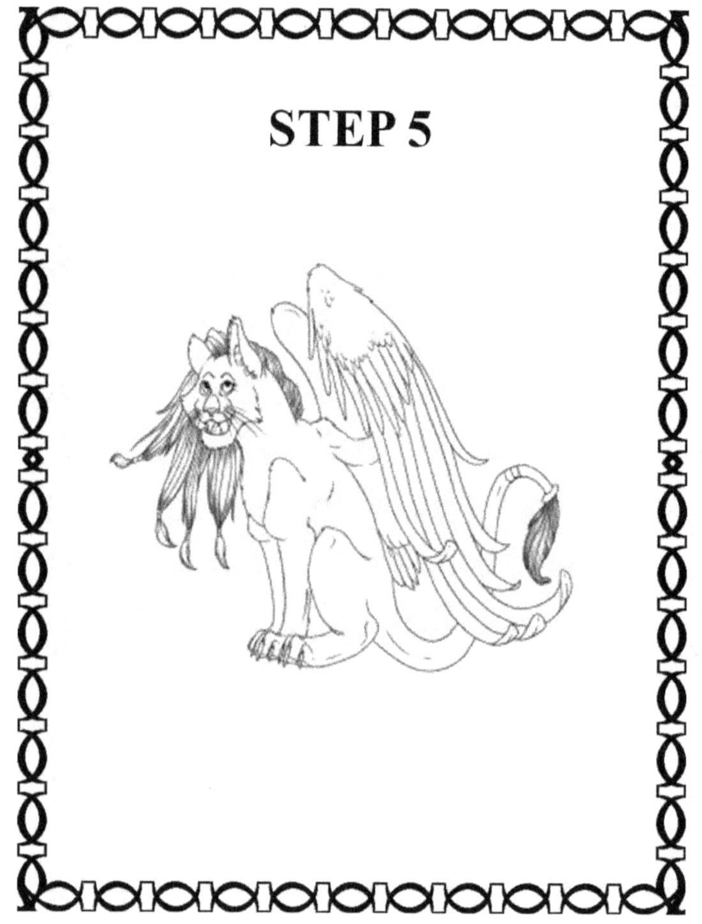
STEP 5

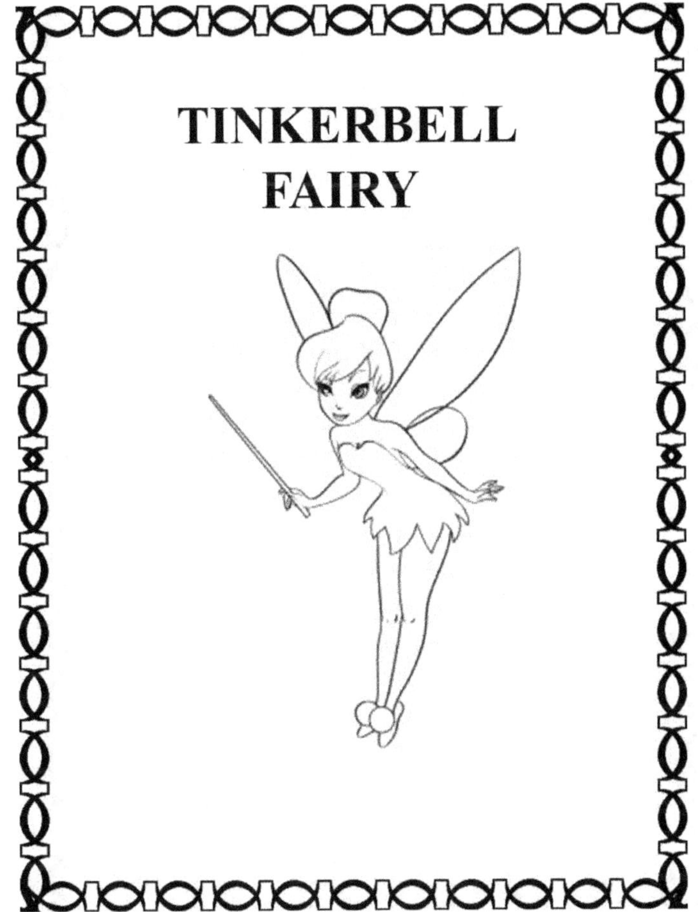
TINKERBELL
FAIRY

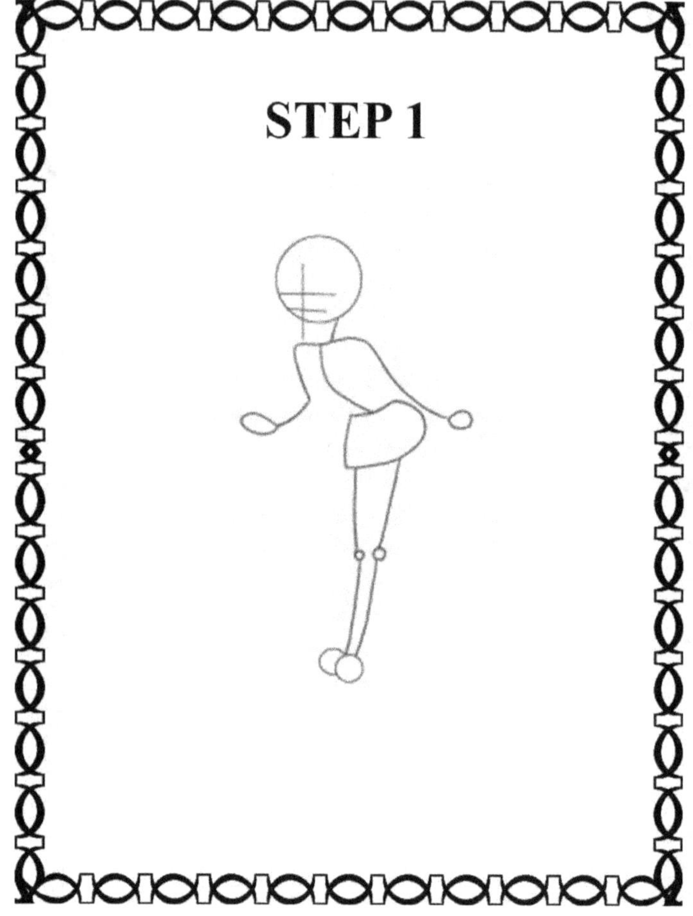
STEP 1

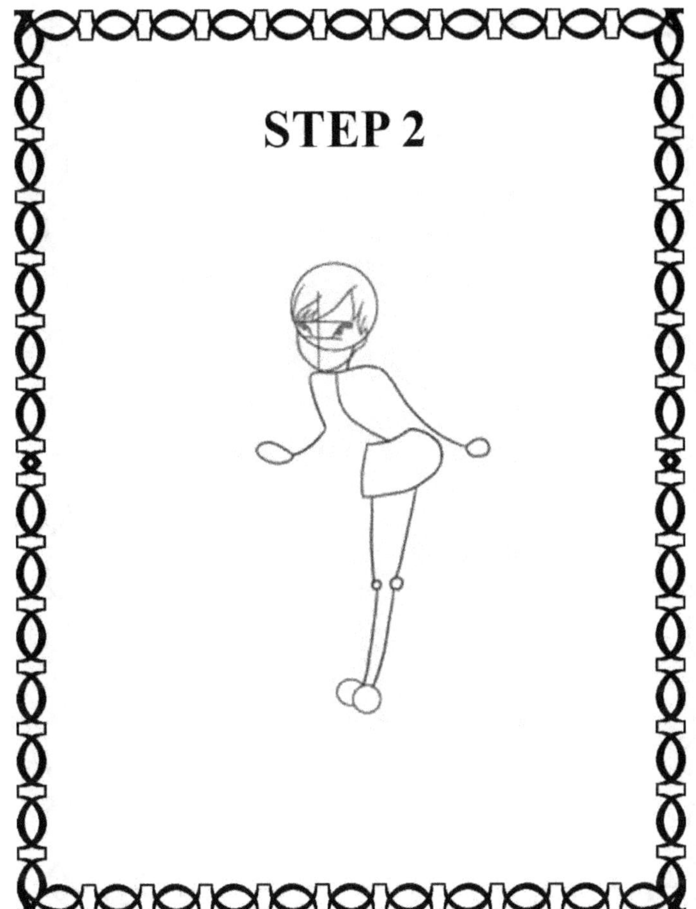
STEP 2

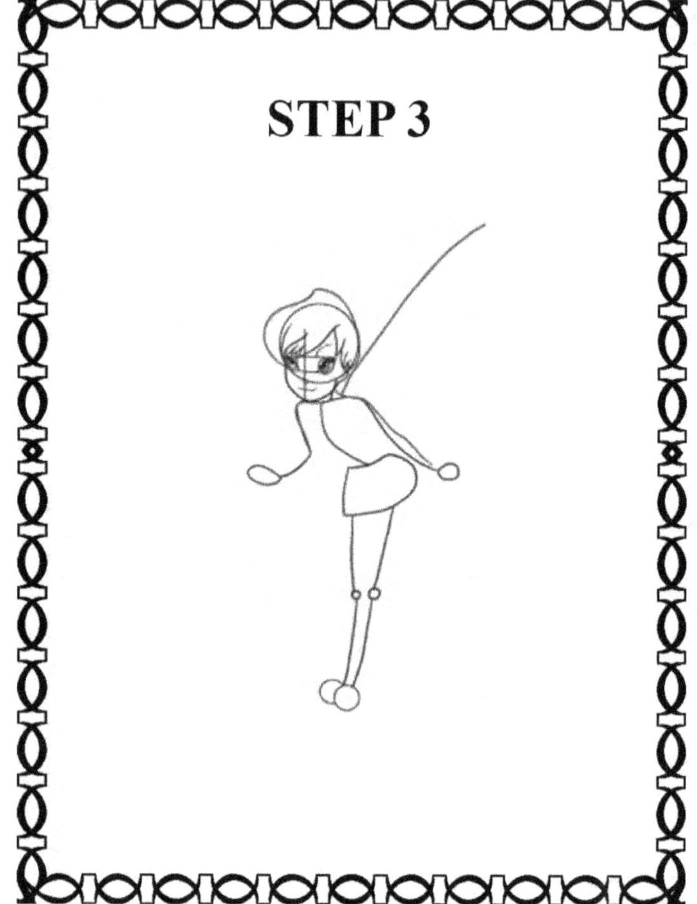
STEP 3

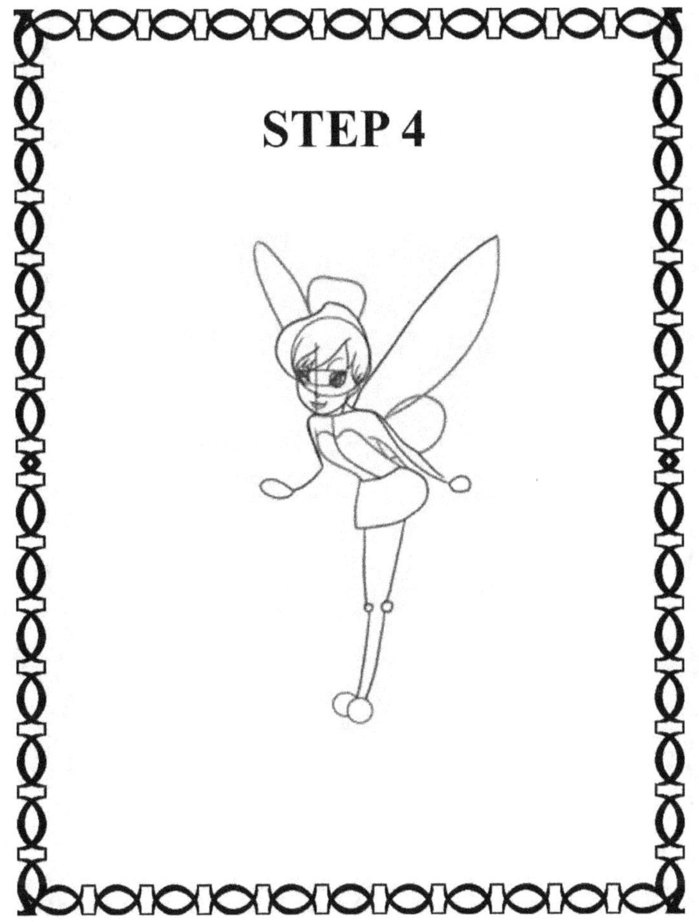
STEP 4

# STEP 5

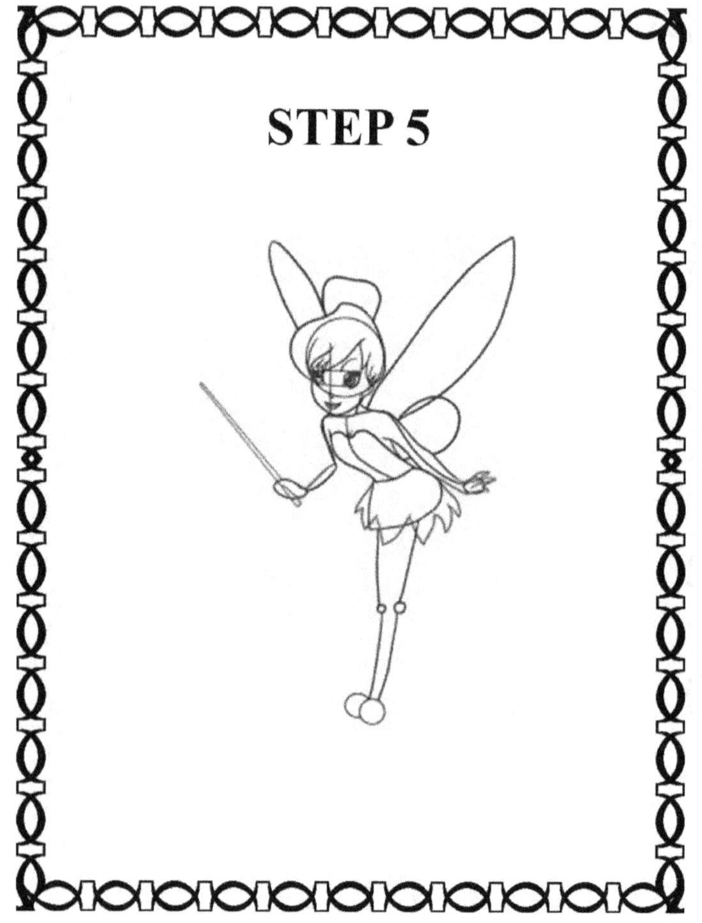

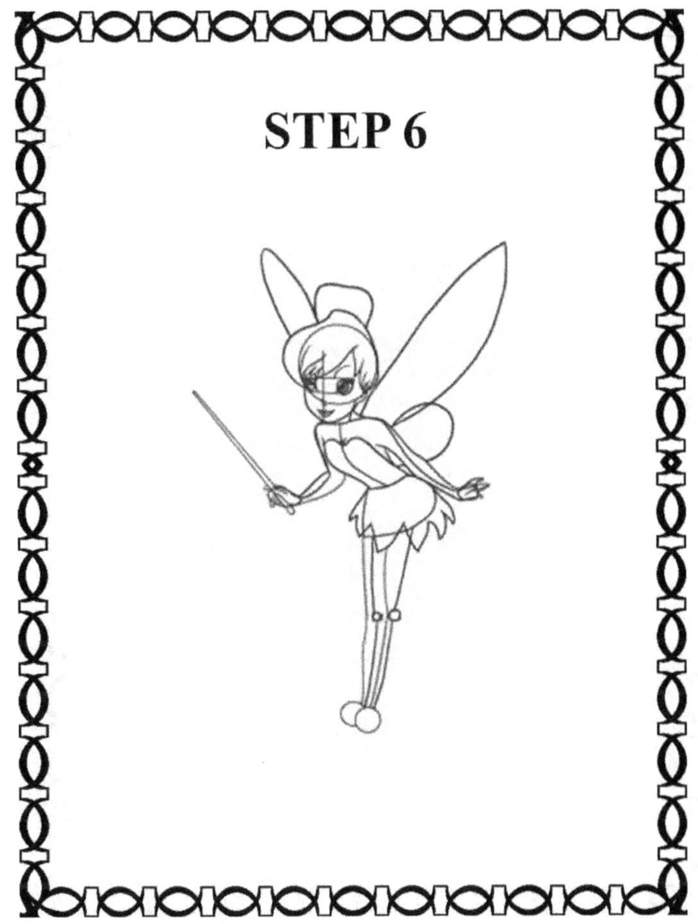
STEP 6

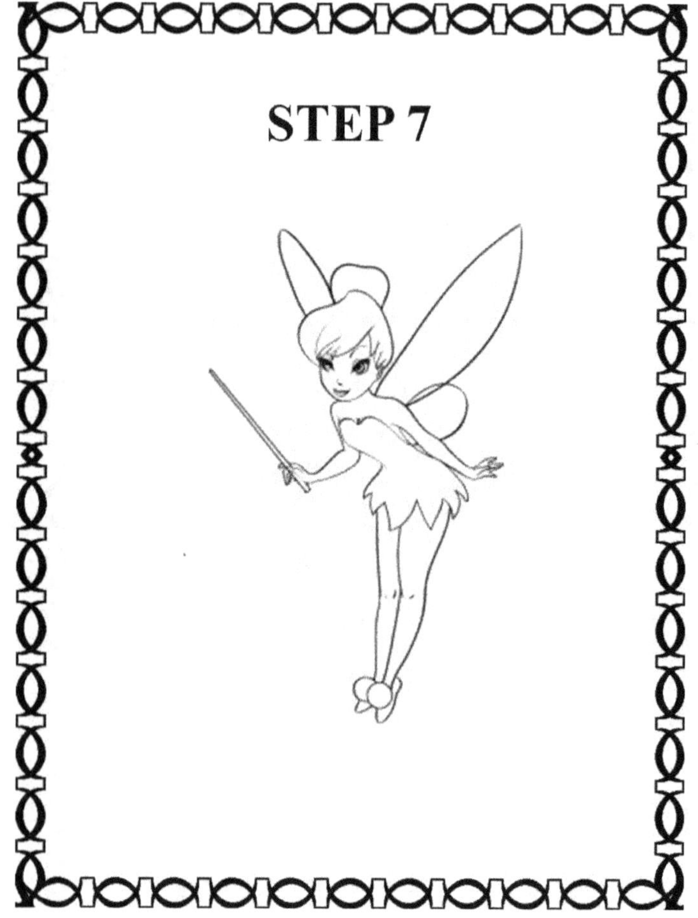
STEP 7

www.ingramcontent.com/pod-product-compliance
Lightning Source LLC
Chambersburg PA
CBHW071649170526
45166CB00003B/1490

* 9 7 8 1 5 2 2 7 0 8 9 6 4 *